Think Like A DJ

7 Steps to Spin Poverty Into Prosperity

Martinez White

DEDICATION

To my first-born son Harlem,

my mother Vanessa and grandmother Olivia,

Dr. Jacqueline DeWalt, Dr. Mercile Lee,

John Wiley, Bob Wynn, Randall, Dave, Andreall

my five siblings,

Julius, Iesha, Dupree "Dee Dee", Isaiah "Zeek", and Ray,

my late father O.C. White,

and the God in you and me.

TABLE OF CONTENTS

FOREWORD I

By Reggie "Smooth Az Butta" Brown

Program Director/DJ at iHeartMedia Milwaukee – 100.7 FM-WKKV – 30-year DJ

One of the things I did while growing up on the east side of Milwaukee, Wisconsin in the late 1970s and early 80s was listen to AM radio. Back then, FM radio was not poppin'. There were only mainstream artists like Madonna dominating FM, while AM was rooted in soul music acts. This was back when we had people picketing outside because we played "Between The Sheets" by the Isley Brothers, and some listeners complained about the lyrics, saying they were too edgy.

There was a Black soul radio station called WAWA 1590 AM. WAWA was home to the best DJs in town and a bunch of powerful on-air talent and cultural personalities, such as radio pioneers like Jimmy Good Times, Steve Haywood, and Dr. Bop, just to name some of my favorites. There was also this one special guy I got a chance to intern with at just fifteen years old, during my time at Marshall and Riverside High Schools. He was my number one idol. His name was O.C. White. He was a legend to me.

Now, I didn't get paid any money back in those days, and I had to spend money to catch the bus everywhere in order to work in the business. I worked for free because all I

1

wanted to be was the best, like O.C. I lived on the eastside, so I had to catch the city bus all the way across town early every Saturday morning. My ride took two hours. I had to change buses three time to get to 128th and Bluemound Road on the southwest side. It was a lot of work, but I had to get there before O.C.! In fact, the bus didn't even stop at 128th Street. I had to get off four blocks earlier on 124th and stop at the Open Pantry convenience store to make sure O.C. had his morning donuts. He turned the station on every morning at 8 a.m., and I was right there with him as his personal assistant.

Ten minutes before he was to crack the microphone and start his show, here came a big, ole green, limousine-style Lincoln Town Car, rushing through the parking like a bat out of hell. Despite there being many parking spots available, O.C. would pull right up to the door and park slightly on the grass, rushing to be on time. Sprinting into the station, he'd grab the hot coffee I'd just made. Then, he'd settle in and take his listeners on a ride over the airwaves. I looked up to Dr. Bop, but not like O.C. because he was from right here in Milwaukee!

O.C. was a true boss. I would see him Friday night at a concert and Saturday morning in the same suit. One of his most unique characteristics was his work ethic. Nobody outworked O.C., which made my job important and interesting. Before he arrived, I would pull the music for that day's show, handpicking the records for the day's playlist for each hour, and finally load all the songs and commercial carts, resembling eight tracks, so all he had to do was pick them up and put them in the machine. Pick the records up, put them on the turntable and press play. Although this man wore a suit every day, he taught me so much about the common man and engaging with people. He did everything, from promoting national acts that toured in Milwaukee to owning the O.C. White Soul Club and a BBQ business. He hired a lot of Black people who couldn't get hired due to discrimination and Jim Crow laws. He was a real hustler, and I admired that. He had the gift of gab and could talk to anybody. He could sell you your own suit. O.C. was truly more than a DJ! As a Civil Rights activist and advocate for peace, if something went wrong in the Black community, he was right there, especially for anything involving the youth.

He'd shout out everybody live on Saturday nights over the air, turning the record slightly down just enough to be heard talking over it, which was a new phenomenon back then and hadn't been heard before. They just don't do radio like that anymore! I'd take the bus just to see him broadcast live on location from the old Kohl's Department Store on Teutonia and Capital Drive, Galst Foods, or Pyles Gift Shop. The only word I can use to describe him is *icon*. As a teenager, I didn't realize I was making history with O.C., not until long after he had passed away.

Martinez, to date, people ask me about your father, mainly because you could not come through Milwaukee or any major city in the Midwest, I don't care what kind of entertainer you were, and not see O.C. He could be seen hanging with everybody, including R&B, Funk, Blues legends like the O'Jays, the Spinners, BB King, ZZ Hill, Little Milton, Denise Lasalle, Luther Vandross, Cameo, Patti Labelle, Isaac Hayes, and Frankie Beverly & Maze. The legends were his friends. Oh! Don't mention George Clinton of Parliament Funkadelic! That's O.C.'s main guy. I first met George because he was like O.C's second assistant, almost had to fight him for my job.

Urban legend has it that, one late summer night when people were getting restless at a delayed Sly & the Family Stone SUMMERFEST concert, back when spending $5 to see an act was a lot of money, your dad stopped people from tearing the place up. He calmed the crowd enough so the show could start.

Back then, the Jackson 5 performed at the arena, known as the Mecca. O.C. White was there, promoting the show. I have vivid memories of the Jackson 5 in Milwaukee, trying to escape the crowd by sneaking out the back door of the venue. I was right there, chasing them down with a group of other kids that was filled with mostly screaming girls. Your dad was a pioneer in his own right. Your daddy was so well-respected, he damn near could have been in James Brown's band. He owned the O.C. White Soul Club and invited Black artists of the times like James, who were making movement music, to come to the club and meet the neighborhood kids. Without your father, Midwest music culture would neither be what it was nor what it is today. Needless to say, O.C. was a hustler!

Fast forward fifteen years later, while I'm hosting a local, city-wide talent show at Centennial Hall in Milwaukee, I meet this young kid named Martinez White, who was impersonating Michael Jackson. He did a few shows and won a few times, and he was a damn good dancer. Fast forward ahead fifteen more years and I'm hosting a Hip-Hop concert at Kiss Ultra Lounge in Milwaukee. I was hired by a party promoter from Madison. They mentioned they had already hired a DJ named M.White. I'd never heard of him, but his name sounded familiar, like I'd seen it somewhere before. I had! It was you, the same dancing kid, O.C. White's son!

We talked about how I knew your dad, and to keep it real, it brought a tear to my eye at the end of the night. I couldn't believe it. I told you just how much your late father had done for me, including the rides home, the money I earned by washing and vacuuming that big long Lincoln on Saturday mornings. That man was like a father to me.

Martinez, I've seen you grow in every aspect. You are indeed "O.C. White, Jr." Here I am right now writing the foreword to your debut book. This is an honor.

I worked for your dad starting at fifteen years old, not getting paid a dollar. I just wanted to be the best, like him. Look at me now. I am the Program Director for V100.7 FM, the number one Hip-Hop and R&B station in my market, having charted a radio career for over thirty years between St. Louis, Chicago, and most notably Milwaukee.

After O.C. retired, I used to get harassed by the police, and I got pulled over one day. I was being chased by a cop. My Jaguar was going fast over a bridge, and I knew his red lights were going to get behind me. I got past him. He hit the lights, and I ran! I parked at the station and dipped in the building. I'd driven in the parking lot so quick and pulled an O.C., BAM! Parking in the spot right in front of the door, on the grass.

Martinez, you're a great guy, who respects other people and always thinks positively, no matter what situation you're in. Your dad is looking down on you, smiling, saying, "That's my boy!" We both got that O.C. White in us! God bless you and may you sell one billion copies of your debut book! Your dad is so proud of you and so am I.

FOREWORD II

By David Muhammad

15 Year DJ, Deputy Director, Milwaukee County Department of Health and Human Services, Manhood Development Coach, Nation of Islam- Milwaukee

I first met Martinez White because he was a part of the University of Wisconsin-Madison's PEOPLE Program, where I worked as a summer pre-college camp counselor and workshop facilitator. We would DJ little parties for the young Black and Brown students who had come from Madison and Milwaukee to be introduced to college life. There's always a couple youth who are into music production, know music beyond their years, or who hang around the DJ table and show interest. Martinez was one of those young people, and he knew enough music to be the DJ.

People of African descent have always passed down oral traditions through their rhythms and their elders. Martinez demonstrated a willingness to listen that has become uncommon between generations. Because of the destruction of Black family life that has taken place since the late sixties, there has been a manufactured disconnect between the youth and their predecessors. As a result, respect is mutually earned rather than conferred due to title or experience. We also live in an era where technology has made it easier to access information, making the role of "teacher" or "mentor" less sought after. Martinez has an old soul that I would later find out came from his father, Milwaukee's legendary O.C. White.

O.C. White was more than a DJ. He was often called the "Mayor of Black Milwaukee," especially during the fair-housing marches that took place during the turbulent late sixties. The O.C. White Soul Club gave a creative outlet of expression for the waves of Black Milwaukeeans whose roots came from Mississippi, Arkansas, and Tennessee. This legacy is what is in Martinez's blood. Even though his father transitioned while he was very young, this left a tremendous imprint on his character and personality.

When he became a college student, the calls for big homies like me to DJ slowed down all of a sudden because now the youth had their own DJ on campus. As a member of Alpha Phi Alpha Fraternity, the UW Madison Gamma Epsilon chapter always had a lock on DJs and campus parties. At least, four brothers in the chapter were DJs, and we threw O'Sickness, the biggest party in the state, so there was no question what frat he would pledge. Martinez showed the principles of Alpha as a youth and exemplifies them now as a brother, a scholar, a father, and a community advocate.

Martinez approaches everything with the mindset of a DJ. A DJ doesn't just play music...your phone does that! A DJ is emotionally intelligent and guides behavior. A DJ considers possible scenarios and prepares meticulously, but surrenders to rhythm and instinct to be responsive in the moment. A DJ is the greatest historian because music is a reflection of the thinking of the people at that moment in time. Music literally allows us to transcend, feel, and share a collective experience.

To think like a DJ means to balance extreme self-confidence

with humility. It is possible, after all, to play people's music wrong and totally be remembered as "that guy who ruined the party." It is not just meeting people where they're at, but also being courageous enough to take them where they didn't know they wanted to go.

DJing is one of the best introductions to entrepreneurship because it comes from a pure motivation. You can't be successful if you don't make people happy and bring them together. You have to already feel genuine emotion for people to be able to connect with you. The party starts with you.

INTRO

A great DJ mixes and masters the art of playing music. You are the DJ of your life, and you are also the music. You must equalize yourself to the highest quality frequency of faith and amplify your wavelength of success, not only for yourself, but also for others, so you can rock the party and make life dance for you. If your life were a party, how many would RSVP? Who would fill your dance floor? If you only live once, will your one party become a party of one? Music is what life feels like. What song will your life play?

When a DJ first accepts a gig, they must first ask themselves, "What kind of party will this be?" From this initial question comes introspection. What we are really asking is, am I capable of doing this? Do I have the sonic knowledge to dance these people into a sock-hop frenzy? Have I ever done one of these types of parties before, and if so, how did it go? We want to know if we can do it. Our subconscious mind is both flattered at another human being's genuine request to dance with us and to our tunes. Although we are flattered, we are also imminently fearful of our ability to carry out the order. Somewhere inside, we are profoundly displaced by the idea, wondering if we can do it. We already know people love for us to curate and select static for them. We've seen our magic. Whether it was at Mom's Saturday morning cleaning fests, Saturday night get-togethers, middle school dances, high school graduation parties, family barbeques, reunions, or while creating playlists for our friends, we know, deep down, we are disk jockeys. In essence, we are back for the first time. From this place of fear, we must then move into an equal and opposite, offensive self-talk of supreme belief and self-confidence.

IT'S GOING DOWN: How It All Started

I was admitted to the University of Wisconsin-Madison as a first-generation college student at sixteen years old. Furthermore, I was awarded a full academic scholarship. This allowed me to emerge from what I didn't know, at the time, was domestic poverty, so I couldn't fuck this up. My momma believed in me and trusted me to do whatna' hell she dropped me off to do, which was get an education, something "they" couldn't take away. In fact, she, Ran-G, and my five siblings drove me to campus, dropped me off, and drove back to Milwaukee. I had to get my shit together, and keep it there.

Being a freshmen in college was rewarding, but there was one disheartening truth. I didn't have time to invest in continuing to produce music either every day or on the weekends. Dr. Mercile J. Lee, the founder/director of the Chancellor's Scholars Program, and Dr. Jacqueline DeWalt didn't pave my way to this Big Ten, world-class, research one institution for me to fumble the bag at the bank of opportunity. Both women served as my campus mothers, and just like my mom, Vanessa, and my granny, Olivia, I couldn't disappoint them. I deeply wanted to put smiles on their faces and hear the affirming words, "Good Job, Martinez!"

As a kid who'd lost my father at just four years old, I yearned for my mother's approval. If I could make her proud, I was convinced she would forget that we'd both lost my dad. My dad is O.C. White, one of the first and, arguably, most influential DJs in my hometown, Milwaukee, Wisconsin, during the Civil Rights Era. When radio was popular as the internet is today, my pops was the man on the radio waves. Even to this day, when I mention my dad to old Black folks in my city, their faces light up, and they always have a story to tell about him. Because of this, I had to focus.

I had a legacy to live up to. Although I knew my history, my destiny remained a mystery. I had to create the party I desired my life to be. In doing so, I had to remain steadfast on handling first things first: Don't waste this opportunity to make Mom proud. It could save her life. So I focused on academics as the first order of business during my entire collegiate freshman year by warming up to the come up. In the words of rap artist J.Cole, this would be my story of how I took the guidelines on how to get up off the sidelines. Three women coaches put me in the game, a game I had to win.

I wanted to take all of my family and friends to the championship of life because we were all playing on the same squad. This would be painful. I knew I wouldn't be able to spend six to ten hours a day making beats on Fruity Loops or editing music on Adobe Audition. At the beginning of the semester, Mercile told me, "Three hours per credit," and I had somewhere between twelve to fourteen college credits on my semester schedule, meaning thirty-six to forty-two hours of studying to account for weekly. After all, she did say college was a full-time job. Furthermore, she would dissect my weekly schedule, carefully examining one hour at time, like a scientist observing a petri dish. Mercile didn't play no games, but I knew I was good at playing music, so maybe, just maybe there was hope.

It was the fall of 2007, the first semester of my sophomore year in college. Although I'd been a music producer in high school and a pseudo-rapper as one-half of Intuition Productions Film & Music Group with my best friend and business partner Randall "Ran-G" Hall, I knew for sure I could make beats. And rap. A little. Ran-G always surpassed me with wit, lyricism, delivery, and flow. Nonetheless, I felt like we were Outkast. He was Big Boi, and I was the confident and eccentric Andre 3000. We were a real Aquemini in our teenage years, yet we are both Leos, like my other high school best friend, Dave "Do Wright" Ellington, the human encyclopedia. I was also best friends with Brandon, who would later become DJ B-Mac during our collegiate years. Ran-G had introduced us. Brandon's mom's basement was where my love for playing music was cultivated. I was in high school, and no matter if it was after school or on the weekends, we played music in the basement and stayed busy enough to stay alive and dodge trouble.

In fact, early that semester, I'd recently attended one of my first college parties and had experienced an epiphany. As I watched this DJ trash his set, I heard my inner voice say, "I can do that even better!" And that's all I needed. There it was. I had it! My passion for producing music can be directly transferred into playing music for others, mostly my college friends I'd been in the Pre-college Enrichment Opportunity Program for Learning Excellence (or PEOPLE) Program with all throughout high school! Suddenly, I could hear the sound of myself. I knew, based on all the nights I played music loud in my momma's living room, selecting everything from the O'Jays to Marvin Gaye, Harold Melvin & the Blue Notes, Mary J. Blige, Anita Baker, Barry White, Earth Wind & Fire, the Commodores, the Temptations, Tupac, Biggie, Prince, Michael Jackson, Stevie Wonder, the Ohio Players, Parliament Funkadelic, the Chi-Lites, Sade, Whitney Houston, and a myriad of other masters of sound, I could definitely spin music and rock the party! I was confident. I believed in me more than anyone else.

Wednesday of the following week, after paying my student housing bill for the semester upfront, buying my books, and agreeing to send Mom a couple dollars, I found the closest DJ store, MC Audio, and purchased $1500 worth of DJ equipment from Mike Carlson himself, a veteran DJ and store owner. I had no idea what to buy. I'd only ever played music in my friend Brandon's mom's basement using DJ equipment that Ran-G bought. So Mike showed me everything I would need. I felt so empowered and in control of my destiny, head held high, as I walked out of MC Audio with my purchase. I knew that, this way, I could continue to develop my passion for music and still kill academically, in order to keep my scholarship to get Mom out of the hood. A win win! Worst case, even if I turned out to be a bad DJ, I could, at least, play music for myself on this new equipment. There were so many things to learn on my new set of Technics SL-1200s, microphone, and mixer! So I cashed out on my dream, spent most of the money I saved, with excitement in my every fiber, adrenaline rushing, and slight panic that I'd just spent the most money I'd ever spent in a single transaction. I was kind of tripping, but I was good because I knew my purpose for being on campus would not suffer. In addition, not only did it take me a year to discover how I'd continue to engage with my passion for music in a meaningful way on this new level, I'd also laid a solid academic foundation and built my study skills my entire freshman year. Suddenly, it occurred to me that maybe, just maybe, I would be in a position to be more academically successful because I could provide consistent financial security for myself. Maybe I was in the perfect position to win. I was still in a new environment, but I had to win, at least for those that believed in me.

On top of all this, Mike had cut me a deal! He'd given me everything for $1,200, instead of $1,500. I couldn't say no! Furthermore, I'd already told Rachel Brooks, a diva-stating member of Delta Sigma Theta Sorority, Inc. that I would DJ the first party of the semester for her and all her Delta sorority sisters a week earlier without ever having DJed before. I had no practical experience, never had touched a set of classic turntables, used a DJ mixer or Serato, or blended two songs together. I'd never scratched a record, or installed a stylus. However, I believed in my abilities and that's what I needed most, self-belief.

I was scared, but faithful. Besides, the party was that Saturday. I had no time to be afraid of my destiny. I had three days and three nights to practice. Practice makes progress. Besides, if Rachel Brooks, a respected Delta upperclasswoman on campus, who'd never heard me play music before, believed in me, I knew I could do it! It wasn't every day a Delta woman asked a non-Greek underclassman to rock their Black Greek party. Perhaps, she saw in me what I felt in myself. I knew how to Think Like A DJ.

Thinking like a DJ is about lifestyle design. It's a positive mindset leading you to a desired end goal. Ultimately, it is a philosophy of successful life leadership. In this paradigm, you are in control of your life-party. It means living a remarkable lifestyle of financial freedom. In this new economy, we must monetize our natural gifts, talents, skills and abilities in order to create, at least, seven streams of income. In all our efforts to achieve abundance, it's imperative that we first lay our baseline lifestyle, equalize our midline frequencies of life experiences, and tweak our highs and lows to play our best life-music, ultimately rocking our most successful life-party. Join me on the wavelength of success by using these seven proven steps to trailblaze your unique path from poverty to prosperity. Together, we make the Dream Circle. You are the DJ. You're your own client, and your life is the party. How many will RSVP? You only live once! Will your one party be a party of one?

Think Like A DJ

1

PICK A TEMPO

Decision - (n) a conclusion or resolution reached after consideration

Picking a tempo is about making a decision. It means making a self-commitment to excellence. Every time I DJ, I intentionally start my set with a particular beats per minute. For example, 66 BPMs versus 144 BPMs makes all the difference. Before every set, I must ask myself, "What kind of party is this?" I must know, believe, and understand the intrinsic qualities and elements of the vibe I'm seeking to create. My goal is to see the next six hours of this party by first visualizing the inevitable event to come. Your life is the party. Your lifestyle is the inevitable event to come. You must first visualize the party you want to create.

CREATE YOUR LIFE-PARTY
First, I premeditate my desires, which must marry themselves to the desires of the person who hired me. In life, God is your boss, telling you what the order of each day is. However, most people sabotage themselves by believing that their individual creative desires outshine those of the Ultimate Creator. Fortunately, this isn't the case. Thankfully, we don't have to know every detail of life in order to begin creating our own life-party. Believing this and walking in such faith releases the debilitating pressure of arrogant

perfectionism and egocentric naiveté. As a human being, living in the natural realm, our meager strength alone is insufficient to solely produce our best life-party. Luckily, we are awarded help from the supernatural. Just as God already has a plan for your life, as the DJ of your one party, you must first visualize your life before you actualize it.

BE GRATEFUL

When I take a gig, my first emotion is gratitude. This is exactly the same way you must start your day – with gratitude. I'm grateful merely because someone called me and trusts that I can perform. In this same spirit, while I'm en route to my event, I thank God for the opportunity to play music for people. The fact that I have such trust with another human being gives me the ultimate peace of mind. My sense of duty to carry out the mission of celebration for those in the room, experiencing my selected sounds and voice, speaks volumes to me. Because I am both excited and slightly nervous about the yet unseen, I calm myself with visions of grandeur. My party will be one my client will forever remember. I project images in my mind of the audience being rejuvenated with frequencies of faith in themselves through movement. As people move in my mind, I see Night Life at the Studio by Ernest Watson. I'm blessed to be the reason for their purity and enjoyment, the placidity in their fluid bodies, their ear-to-ear smiles, their eye contact with one another, knee-slaps, high-fives, hugs, embraces, and fidelity to authentic self. My life's work as a jock is to inspire their real-time jolts, straight lines, and coils, like the sonics of a native Kiswahili tongue.

VISUALIZE, THEN ACTUALIZE

Before I even arrive at the venue, I meditate on what is to ensue during my performance. As Shakespeare makes clear, your life is a stage, and all the people in the world are mere players. Your theater is full of seats. Who will fill them to see your movie on the screen? Before I get to the gig, I take my vision of what should happen, couple it with the expectations of my client, and play the party in my head. Then I decide. I pick a song, matched with a beat and flow of melodies I believe mirror my picturization with the explanation of the client's needs. You are your own client. What kind of party do you want your life to be?

SEE THE END FROM THE BEGINNING

As a DJ strategy, for parties with a younger crowd, I usually err toward a slower tempo, usually 80 BPMs or lower, as a start, beginning with a song I know we both will love. For a mature crowd, I typically do the opposite and start with 100 BPMs or better, sometimes even 120. From these epicenters, I work my way to the opposite ends of the slow to fast tempo continuum.

Without picking a tempo or making a decision on where I want to start prior to DJing, I have not pointed my feet in the direction of my destination. If I don't take time to think of the way I must go, I will be lost in my music mix, just as you'll be lost in the mix of life. The first thing anyone does before landing safely on a plane, they must begin with typing their destination. Reverse engineer your success.

Begin with the end goal as your chief thought. Keep it retained in the center of your mind. Where do you want to end up? What is the vision for your style of life? What do you look like, smell like, feel like? In your most successful form, what does the air around you taste like? How do your arms sway in the wind and the heels of your feet and tips of your toes alternate on the pavement? What kind of ground do you stand on? Are you standing tall, with relaxed shoulders, walking in warm sunshine, or are you kneeling in a private sunny garden, sifting through the soil, winnowing through the weeds? What visions are playing on the screen during the movie in your head that no one can see, but you and God? What does it feel like to be successful and fulfilled?

In your own words, describe your dream vision:

_____

_____

_____

_____

_____

_____

_____

_____

_____

_____

_____

_____

_____

_____

_____

_____

_____

_____

_____

_____

_____

_____

_____

_____

_____

_____

Is that all? Did you miss any details?

_____

_____

_____

_____

_____

_____

_____

_____

_____

_____

_____

_____

_____

DREAMS ARE MADE TO BE ACHIEVED™

This exercise may prove to be a difficult one if you've never asked yourself what you want for yourself. You may find yourself feeling frustrated because you must be accountable to yourself and because you must challenge yourself. By simply having a dream, one feels obligated to achieve it. That's completely okay, dreaming can create a kind of anxiety. This is what the late U.S. Congressman John Lewis meant by "good trouble." Our dreams have weight, and we are all strong enough to carry them from ideation to creation.

My personal life motto and mantra is "Dreams Are Made To Be Achieved" ™, and it has helped me with mitigating my dream anxiety since I was twelve years old. Upon founding my company, Intuition Productions, I needed a bold statement of accountability that was inspiring and invigorating yet healing. One day, in high school, while making beats and recording songs in a make-shift studio in my sister's closet, I had an epiphany. It was like a warm ray of sun shining through a thundercloud. "Dreams Are Made

To Be Achieved" ™ is an all-encompassing statement. It foretells the future of my success by its syntactic structure. A dream is achieved because it is first, well, achievable. A dream is achievable not merely because it was made, but because it was created to be such.

For instance, why would a four-year-old kid believe in being an astronaut if they first didn't believe it was even possible? We dream what we inherently know we are capable of manifesting. I believe in this dream statement so much that, the moment I turned eighteen, I had it tattooed over my heart, forever canonized. It not only serves as my personal mantra and instantaneous affirmation; it is also my company motto. What is your powerful dream statement? What is a phrase or affirmation that can, with one utterance, amplify your input frequency to your highest level of desired output in life? What will you say to yourself to jolt you into a realm where nothing is impossible by simply using an affirmation?

Growing up, having lost my father at just four years old to a premature death in 1994, I had to create internal peace of mind. I am one of many Black adults recovering daily from early childhood trauma. Although I've heard a plethora of stories about my father's vitality as one of the first Black and most influential Civil Rights era DJs, I only have a handful of personal memories I carry in my heart. That threshold is sealed with all the unforgettable times he took me to Burger King, bought me my first bike, pointed and winked, or dropped off a surprise. He and my mom weren't married. In fact, he was married to another woman, from whom he was separated, but as a toddler, I thought I was the only person in the world that mattered to him. My oldest brother Ray and I were his main concerns. Pops took good care of us, and we knew it. This is why I significantly value my relationship with my own son Harlem.

Harnessing this depth of conscious and subconscious anger, defeat, disenchantment, turmoil, and grief, I knew, at twelve years old, that I had to create a dream statement that would, by vocalization, dwarf the pain I was surviving, due to the early childhood trauma of losing my dad. I needed a dream statement strong enough to set me straight any time I felt really low. Although I've seen therapists since right after I lost my dad, I inherently knew I had to conjoin my deepest self-commitment to excellence with a statement powerful enough to serve as instant therapy. So there it was: "Dreams Are Made To Be Achieved" ™ It's similar to "ask and you shall receive," or "seek and you shall find." "DAMTBA" ™ is a self-pact that, no matter the calamity or circumstance, no one can delete your work ethic, the currency exchange for your dreams. The dream is free, a gift from God, yet the hustle demands work ethic. Faith without work is dead. We work because we believe.

WHAT IS YOUR DREAM STATEMENT?

_____

_____

_____

_____

_____

_____

_____

_____

_____

_____

_____

_____

_____

_____

_____

_____

_____

_____

_____

_____

_____

_____

_____

_____

_____

_____

KEEP YOUR EYES ON THE PRIZE

My mom raised six children without a lot of help. I didn't know I was growing up in poverty until I emerged from it as a sixteen-year-old college admit. When I first stepped foot on campus, certain microaggressions and signposts told me I was in an unfamiliar space, living in a foreign place. Other freshmen had cell phones, cars, two parents that dropped them off, a dorm room full of all kinds of food, drinks, and snacks, and they were seemingly more familiar with study habits and prerequisite curriculum fundamentals. Here I was, having graduated as salutatorian of my class, senior class president, student council president, and prom king, and I didn't have an abundance of the monetary resources and educational cultural capital. I was surprised at how far my public education had left me behind. However, I knew I had to make a choice. Was I going to blow my opportunity and return to poverty? Would I get so distracted by the reputation of UW-Madison being the #1 party school in the Big Ten that I'd have to forfeit my full-ride academic scholarship? Would I piss away my biggest dream to date of emerging from my hood and being an example to my four younger siblings? Would I fumble the chance to pay Moms back for all the love she had wrapped around me after my dad left us? Would I disappoint my granny? Would I make Mercile and Jackie look bad? Would I mess up the church's money? I couldn't. Plus, my best friend Dave was my roommate and my accountability partner from home, while Ran-G checked in on me all the time from Milwaukee and eventually   Arizona.

PICK A TEMPO: Make A Decision

If your life was a party, you must first pick a tempo! How fast or slow will you begin your journey in order to arrive at your desired destination? Will you self-select layovers or have a direct flight to the airport of success for which you've dreamt? Pick a place to start, seeing the end goal from the beginning. Just like when I walked on campus at sixteen years old, claim your prosperity, despite your humble beginnings. Create a success consciousness by first carefully crafting your Dream Statement. This is the inception of your wealth. Remember, it's something you'd feel compelled to tattoo over your heart, literally or figuratively. Make your life-party a priority. When your life ends, you should know exactly what people will say about you because, every day, in every facet of your life, you are creating the story they will tell. You are the DJ for the party they will experience. I know how many will RSVP to my party, do you?

YOU WILL IMPACT CULTURE FOREVER

Furthermore, it's imperative for you to visualize your life as a majestic Pyramid of Giza. Would you want to impact culture in a similar fashion for the next 4,000 years? Do you want people, hundreds of generations from now, to know you once lived in the synapse of time? People need to talk about your party forever!

First, you must create the memorable experience they will have conversations about, that professors will teach about, at which young children will marvel, gazing in amazement. "How?" you ask. You must build a remarkable life.

DID YOU KNOW YOU'RE WORTH $85 BILLION?

According to Dr. Dennis Kimbro's mind-building book Think & Grow Rich: A Black Choice, "researchers now calculate that if the electronic energy of the hydrogen atoms in the human body could be utilized, a single person could supply the electrical needs of a large, highly industrialized country for nearly a week." One noted theorist claimed that the atoms in our bodies contain a potential energy charge of more than eleven million kilowatt hours per pound; in effect, the average person, by this estimate, is worth $85 billion." With a B. If you're just average, you're worth 85 Bs, and you're not average, by far! Is it possible you could be worth much more?

Money, known as "currency", has an electric flow. Wealth attracts itself. In our new economy, working-class people must first create a wealth consciousness in their efforts to achieve financial freedom. They must elevate their understanding of how currency accumulates, is protected, preserved and distributed in life, or left for legacy purposes, in death. In order to emerge from poverty to prosperity, one must possess a burning desire for financial freedom, coupled with a money consciousness backed by faithful persistence.

The universal law of attraction dictates that like-energies, frequencies, and wavelengths of thought shall draw all other forces of similar facets. What we think most manifests. From a thought-space comes physical action. Upon alignment with a residual, ritualistic exchange of sweat equity, these actions will transform your abstract dreams from the synthetic realm to a concrete physical equivalent.

Behold, a new reality! The one you dreamed of!

Our inner enthusiasm, merely by the nature of our humanity, gives us the power to create our destiny. We know our personal history, yet what's ahead? What's our personal destiny? Luckily, we can create it. That's the fun part! The Ultimate Creator, God endowed us with the gift of dominion. Unlike animals, we can absolutely create our reality. Our inner enthusiasm umbilically connects us to all our God-given gifts, talents, skills and abilities, which pave our road to financial sustainability, yielding intergenerational economic impact. It is only when we learn to listen to that inner-self, barely as loud as a whisper to us, that we can begin to direct our natural-born enthusiasm, completely igniting the law of attraction. We have the power to yield a monetary equivalent in direct proportion to the depth of our commitment toward achieving all the burning desires of our heart.

CREATE A VISION BOARD

Challenge yourself to elevate your wealth conscious by first acknowledging you're in control of your destiny in a free-enterprise society. Living in Kenya, the developing world for six months, at just 19 years old, I realized the privilege of living in a first world country. The resources and infrastructure available to Americans is remarkable and gives rise to countless rags to riches stories of enterprise. Feel the power of self-control in this environment, especially if you're of an emerging community or emerging ethnic background. As a Black American, your ancestors died for your freedom. Someone's name you'll never know, exchanged his or her life with hope of your appreciation. You have such an incentive to participate in the economic opportunities of America. Society has a debt owed to you paid for by someone else's life in your bloodline and family tree. Reason why there's so much covert and overt resistance to stop you, literally or figuratively, dead in your tracks. Like the speed of sound, the faster you go, the more resistance you experience as the object in motion. Get ready for a sonic boom. A transcendence. In moments of self-doubt, self-pity or despair, due to acts of resistance, know you are already rich, no wonder the enemy of peace desires to destroy your joy. No sense in robbing a poor man and you're so rich. Your spirit is gold. Your worth is incalculable. You are bountiful and limitless. Your ingenuity is a threat to those who take it as such. In these times, Dr. Kimbro proclaims self-talk will be your key to the machine of achievement. Connection will be your key to the door of abundance. Plug yourself up to the electric current of success. Imagine yourself building new realities in your mindspace. Next, see intense belief fanning your flames of desire. Now, it's clear you want financial independence bad enough, but how BIG do you want it? What does financial independence look like, feel, taste and sound like to you? Write it down, and it shall manifest. At once! Envision yourself donning your success, wearing it like a sacred cloak.

Create a physical vision board of beautiful cutout magazine and newspaper images that strike your primal success barometer. Trust your instincts. Choose images that naturally move you. Be intentional. Every image must reflect how it would feel to design the lifestyle you desire. Post it in a place you will see every day, preferably a living room wall. Repeat this as often as the season changes. At this point, you've picked your tempo.

2

DROP YOUR FIRST RECORD

"Faith is the head chemist of the mind." - Napoleon Hill

Dropping your first record requires *actionable faith*. According to the Word of God, faith is the evidence of things unseen, yet the substance of things hoped for. What do you see? What are you hoping for? Based on your own personal vision board, what image of success have you painted as your desired lifestyle? Even more importantly, are you willing to act on what you now know to be true from chapter one, the fact that success is yours to hold? Have you crafted a powerful mantra you can repeat to yourself in the times of compromising defeat? Furthermore, are you making enough deposits in this vision in order to make equal and opposite withdrawals, ultimately extracting your desired lifestyle? Most of us check our bank account balance daily and, sometimes, multiple times per day on our phones. Why don't we check the bank of life in this same fashion? In order to withdraw our desired lifestyle, we must make daily faithful deposits of sweat equity.

WE ARE ALL ONE

Everything that exists undergoes two creations. First, in the supernatural realm, there is a hunch or a spark of imagination. Then, in the natural realm, there is a physical equivalent that we can touch or experience. Much like when we have decided on our tempo, a predetermined vision, we must then *drop our first record* in accordance with our efforts to *rock the party*. A key difference is we must couple our own desired tempo with that of God's own desires for our lives. We must listen before, during, and after we play our first song. What good does it do to pick a tempo, have a song cued and never even play one record? Just like a successful DJ must play his first song, our imagination must pursue action, or no one will get an opportunity to hear our music. Even worse, the pain your music was designed to take away from the audience it serves will instead prevail, leaving them to parish, unhealed. Because you didn't live out your dreams, those around you, who are inextricably linked to you and your dream, are not as empowered or rightly equipped with the best tools to achieve theirs. We are all connected. Before we're born, all our friendships and connections are predestined. Perhaps, God coupled me with Dave, Ran-G, Brandon, and Mike for an ultimate, greater purpose. There's not a single fiber of insignificant energy on this earth, including the energy that you bring to this planet. By you simply having breath in your body, you are important to God, for each of us serves a purpose as a different part of the sum of the body of Christ. Consequently, no one individual can move independently without contorting other parts of this fully functioning body. Ran-G may be the arm of Christ, helping us all reach new depths in our Dream Circle, while Dave could very well be functioning as the cerebral cortex, guiding us. Brandon may serve as Christ's feet, marching us ahead, while Mike could very well be serving as a light unto my path toward artistic enlightenment. Inevitably, we each have a part to play, impacting other people. God has predestined our friendships.

What's your role? Perhaps your destiny is mathematically linked to those around you in a preconceived fashion, even before the beginnings of Earth itself? Since it actually is, we all need you to self-actualize so that we may do the same. We are one.

WHAT TUNE WILL YOUR LIFE PLAY?

Jump and the net will appear. Perhaps, your steps are already ordered by the Ultimate Creator, who has the best picture for your life already painted. If you don't jump, you'll forever stand on the cliff of possibility, forfeiting the opportunity to experience the adrenaline rush of achieving impossibility. Everything is impossible until it isn't. For there has been no one thing that has always been, but God. For everything we can conceive has been created from nothingness. A light bulb was once candlelight. A lifestyle was once a dream. The concrete was once abstract. All physical matter was once synthetic. Per Napoleon Hill, our world has emerged from the creative faculty of the inventors' imagination. Thomas Edison once confessed, "I have not failed. I've just found 10,000 ways that won't work." What attempt to create your life-party are you on? What is your candlelight idea you want to capture in a filament, eternally illuminating and impacting culture? What song for your life do you desire to leave behind?

BEGIN AT ONCE

Deep down inside, we all want to be important or significant in the eyes of others, yet you must have one success in order to have two. Start small, like I did the night I DJed my first gig with the Deltas. Start at once, whether you feel 100% prepared or not. Start by identifying your destination. What's your place of arrival? Where do you want to go? After you've identified the type of music your client wants, start playing songs aligned with those wishes. Just as one would ask passengers to board a plane prior to getting it in the air, gather the necessary itinerary, because soon, you'll be flying. Don't forget, you're your own client.

Dropping your first record is about taking your destiny into your own hands and walking in your calling. Take your first steps in the direction your gift is pulling you. To stay the course, I suggest you hold in your mind a crystalized vision of only your most successful self. Only visualize positive images, feelings, emotions, sounds, and insights. To assist with steadfastly existing in this state of powerful obsession, I will ask you to do two simple things – write your vision daily and repeat your dream statement seven times during your daily activities.

WRITE YOUR VISION: DO YOU HAVE FIFTEEN MINUTES FOR SUCCESS?

Every night, immediately before you retire to bed, set your phone's stopwatch for fifteen minutes. Affix the Do Not Disturb or Airplane Mode feature and write, non-stop, whatever vision comes to mind of your most successful self. What does your successful self look and feel like? What activity are you doing, and how does it feel to be the best you, the person you were born to be? What is the most successful version of you in your deep consciousness? Don't pause to think. You should be writing so fast that the next word is difficult to predict, yet it comes out fluidly, completing a story. If you know what's next in your mind, before your hand actually writes it on the page, you're not giving yourself permission enough to free write. Don't go with the flow. Be the flow. Soon the words you use will be writing themselves, placing themselves in the perfect order, telling your most intimate vision of success. Continue to write, even if your hand hurts or you start feeling as though you're running out of words. You conquer these physiological misfortunes by, yep, you guessed it, continuing to write! Seven minutes might feel like fifteen, so don't stop until your stopwatch clock alarm rings at fifteen. Then, immediately, within five minutes of wrapping up, prepared for your night's rest, lie in bed and go to sleep. Allow yourself to fall asleep naturally.

SEVEN: THE NUMBER OF COMPLETION

Upon waking up in the morning, prior to checking all your social media platforms, emails, missed calls or text messages, repeat your dream statement seven times with the kind of enthusiasm, passion, and fervor one would state, "NOT GUILTY" to a crime they didn't commit. Repeat this self-homework, daily, as often as you brush your teeth.

I will write my vision daily because:

_____

_____

_____

_____

_____

_____

_____

_____

_____

_____

_____

_____

I speak & repeat my personal dream statement 7 times because:

_____

_____

_____

_____

_____

_____

_____

_____

_____

_____

_____

_____

As a writer, you must write. As a performer, you must perform. You already are who you desire to be. Your form simply needs to physically manifest through actionable faith. Just as a DJ must, during every party, we all must *drop our first record* for our own life party. If you have a business idea, *begin at once*, whether you have everything you feel is necessary to get started or not. If you have a book inside you, *start writing*! If you want to be the first person in your family to go to college and graduate, affix your feet in the direction of your dream. If you want a promotion, *plan and execute*! Where's your itinerary? What's your destination? Are you on the plane or still sitting in Terminal B? Turn against any and all destructive pathways antithetical to excellence. Focus your thoughts, feelings, words, actions and emotions on only what you most desire. Your commitment will manifest the truest desires of your heart. For what you want most shall appear. It's the law of attraction.

MANIPULATE TIME TO YOUR BENEFIT

I earned my Emmy Award for Outstanding Children's Programming by *dropping my first record*. Because time seemed to be wasted in my neighborhood, I manipulated time to my benefit, using every nanosecond of it to make progress or build symbiotic relationships. If I was going to be bored by simply not having enough to do or places to go, the least I could do was use my time wisely, manipulating it to pay me a dividend, ultimately, for the betterment of my life and my Dream Circle. This way, time would be my friend versus my sworn enemy. Boredom suddenly became an opportunity. When you're at the bottom, the only direction you can go is up. We all have time to get ahead. However, most people use the limited time they already have complaining about their lack, which amplifies the negative thoughts screaming in their head, infecting their attitude with corrosive defeat, before they ever even try.

This won't be you. That trap is old. You are now more enlightened and more woke than ever. As a middle and high school kid, I knew the tenacity inside me outweighed the excitement around me. There was not much constructive happening in my neighborhood on Fifteenth and Keefe Avenue for a twelve-year-old. Because I believed dreams were meant to be achieved, I knew it was only a matter of time between the lifestyle I was born into and the lifestyle I would live. More importantly, I knew I possessed the strength and wherewithal to make it happen, and I knew that God would be there with me, while also sending me people in the natural realm, like Dave and Ran-G, who would serve as wind at my back, instead of at my face. Persistence versus resistance. I was failing forward, fast and frequently, in all efforts to learn how to fly from crawling.

CAN YOU LOOK AWKWARD FOR YOUR DREAM?

Every day, obsessing over this belief of achieving my dream, I spent time after school, during my middle and high school years, at a local community learning center or Saturday morning school program. I wasn't afraid of looking awkward. I knew I was one of the only kids hanging around school on the weekends or staying with the teachers after we were all dismissed for the day. I was not fearful of being viewed as eccentric or a little off-center. Other kids wouldn't dare get to school early or leave later because of an opportunity to host the morning announcements or record a TV show. That was too corny or boring to most kids during my formative years. What I learned was, despite what the masses do, we, as DJs, must get out of our comfort zones. To be a successful jock, we must be the most comfortable in our own *uncomfortability*. We have to trust ourselves to drop a record, one we may have never heard before. Despite this being its first spin, we must trust that, if this song doesn't resonate with our audience, we have the next, better record, cued and ready to drop to reclaim the positive energy in the room. After we decide on our tempo, we can move into our first actionable step of possibly looking awkward and *dropping our first record*. In essence, we must go to school on Saturday. We must walk faithfully into who we were created to be! Maybe, just maybe, that's what people want from us most, our authentic selves. Don't be scared! Even if you still are, *drop your first record*! After all, we want to feel your beat!

3

FEEL THE BEAT

*"Connection is the key to the door of abundance." -
Anonymous*

Feeling the beat is about connection. As a performance DJ, we must connect with the science of motivating people to dance. Feeling the beat entails catching a groove in your mix that displays a depth in music wisdom and breadth in sonic creation. Once you've dropped your first record, it's important to match the energy of that record with your subsequent fifteen to thirty minutes of songs. You want to warm yourself up to the room and vice versa.

WHAT IS YOUR DJING STYLE?
Feeling the beat is the act of acquainting your audience with your style of play. Do you mix, scratch, and blend songs well? Do you let songs play a while or mix a new record after every first verse? Can you beat match well? Do you use sound effects, or do you talk on the microphone? Obtaining your audience's trust is vital and requires connection. That connection dictates the depth of music experimentation you are capable of doing during your set, while retaining your audience's interest, and it underlines the level of your crowd's enjoyment. Without your audience's trust, you are void the ability to surprise, engage, or entertain them,

inevitably losing their suspension of disbelief. Luckily, consistent connection serves as a confidant. You build reverence from your audience by earning their rapport. You must play music and, in real time, evaluate if your audience is feeling your set. If not, luckily you can change it right away because you are the DJ and this is your party!

HOW FANTASTIC IS YOUR VOYAGE?

While in the mix on the wheels of steel, a DJ must connect with their audience with a surgeon's accuracy. Connecting requires you to constantly cycle through an act, listening, and evaluation rotation of thought. Thinking like a DJ requires all parts of your brain to activate. Laziness is our enemy. We have no time to slack. Most times, we only have minutes before songs are over, and we must keep the music going. We cannot self-sabotage by mixing songs we know are not crowd-pleasers or being so arrogant in our mix that we alienate those we're hired to please. We've all been to a party where the DJ sounds like they're playing for themselves and not you, the partygoer. As a DJ, our entire spirit must be nonjudgmentally open in order to feel the energetic nuances in the room. We must be emotionally intelligent and selflessly care about the enjoyment of others enough that we evaluate our performance in the moment. We are but a vessel of creativity and a ark pitched toward euphoria of how every many people decided to join us that night on a fantastic voyage. Who's dancing on the boat with you during your successful years?

PLAY TO YOUR AUDIENCE

People are most attracted to the kind of songs a DJ picks. How many times have you left a party saying, "That DJ played my song"? Uniqueness in a DJ's song curation sets them apart from their peers and can bend time or even give it a stopping sensation, creating a memorable moment for your crowd. Yes, people like the tricks of turntablism, yet are most appreciative of you playing their favorite tunes, in an exciting order. Trusting that song order is riding the wave, which we will take time to explore in the next chapter. In order to give yourself the best possible chance to have a party as awe-inspiring as the Pyramids of Giza, we must connect with our audience through a diverse song selection threaded by continuity. Without a continuous, fluid flow of frequencies, our output has no thematic element, ultimately lacking impact. The best DJs know they are servants to their audience. Define your continuum of success. Who are you trying to serve?

In the workforce, perhaps your audience is your co-working staff and management team. Feeling the beat on the job or in your own business may involve a probationary two- to five-year period or, in some cases, as short as sixty to ninety days. This is where you are building a connection with those around you. In this brief time, people get to know your morals, ethics, and values. Here, your character becomes beknown. These foundational connections will serve you your entire life. Your network is your net worth! Who you know will get you in the door. What you know will keep you there! Furthermore, those who know you will protect your reputation when you're not in the room. Build genuine connections with people who will stand up for you during your absence. Create advocates, so even in the event negativity tries to discredit you when you're not around, righteousness will speak up through someone else's voice who is compelled to tell their positive personal story about you. Who knows you will protect your energy, even when you're not present to defend yourself. When dark energy starts to swarm your light in a room, righteousness shall object, illuminating your authenticity and positivity like an ultra-light beam, shielding your reputation from eclipsing collateral damage. Have you equipped people enough with the stories they will tell about you? Have you gotten in the groove of your life record, or is there so much static that even others can't hear the song you're trying to play? I believe in you and your dream, and so should you. Do you feel your own beat? Does it connect well with others?

I have the following 7 naturally unique passions, gifts, skills, talents or abilities:
1.
2.
3.
4.
5.
6.
7.

Describe 7 practical ways to generate income streams from your 7 passions, gifts, skills, talents or abilities:
1.
2.
3.
4.
5.
6.
7.

4

RIDE THE WAVE

Radical Trust - (n) confidence in the unseen or inevitable

Riding the wave means sustaining radical trust, while you're in the mix of life. DJs, at every performance, exercise deep trust in themselves. No matter what, they approach the turntables knowing instinctively when to mix or remix a song. They know they will keep music flowing, continuing to play tunes they believe will build enough rapport with their audience the party vibe eventually operates on autopilot. During this transition from *feeling the beat* to *riding the wave*, the performance mission suddenly shifts from needing to create a flow to sustaining it.

In our lives, we all reach a point during our personal development where we are most focused on answering big, internal questions. Abysmal questions with no finite answer. We may ask questions like: What do I want to do for a living? Why am I alive? What will my impact be? We question if what we're doing every day in life will actually get us to where we're trying to go. Equivalent to turbulence on a flight, we may, in fact, experience turbulent times during our DJ sets.

After all, we are flying. Just as in life, we may start with a goal in mind, only to be sidetracked by something we could not predict or foresee. Here is where we must *ride the wave*.

SEEK PROBLEM VS. SOLUTION BINARIES

We must learn to troubleshoot, while simultaneously keeping the movement moving. Just as every DJ must prevent dead air during their set, you must uphold personal trust in yourself and the insights God shared with you about the plan for your life. You have built your audience, so play the music you know they love to hear. Don't settle for discouragement when things don't go as planned; instead, change during the process or alter it altogether. After all, every good DJ knows the word *troubleshooter* is a synonym for the term *DJ*. We are natural problem solvers. Our natural knack is to be results-driven, solution-oriented creatures of habit. If a needle breaks, a song gets mistakenly unloaded from our deck, or a software program crashes, we must have a solution prepared. Do you have a backup needle, another song already cued up, or an auxiliary plug to play a song request you've never heard from someone in your audience? Misfortunes will arise. The unexpected will inevitably happen, but that's what gives your life-party twists, turns, dead ends, restarts, resurrections, and remixes. The ingenuity required to respond to troubleshooting while in the mix is what *riding the wave* feels like. It's exhilarating. This resourcefulness in a time of need, while upholding a standard of excellence in our DJ set gives us a sense of exuberance. This high-level of self-awareness creates resilience and ensures we become stronger in our craft by way of muscle memory. When we learn a new DJ tactic, we know it forever. Similar to when you become emotionally intelligent in an area or pick up a new skill, credential or license, you retain that wisdom over time.

For instance, usually when I spin a party, at least, three

to five small things always happen that I could not have predicted before I started my set. Some common things that happen include one of my earphones not working properly, a cable having an electric shortage, the area where I'm planning to DJ is too far from a power source on a wall perimeter, the wedding client changed their first dance song, or I didn't have a song someone requested. As an experienced DJ, I expect and am mentally prepared for delays, detours, or unforeseen circumstances because, no matter what, the show must go on. I must go with the flow and respond to turbulence, while in flight. Don't stop the music.

ANXIETY CAN'T STOP YOU

When I first started DJing, just as I remember as a kid, unexpected change would create anxiety for me during my set. As a fatherless young boy, I hated to leave my mom because losing my dad was traumatic enough. At five, I remember my first day of school. My mom dropped me off, and naturally, I cried because I didn't want to leave her, considering my father had seemed to disappear to a new state or something. I didn't know. I felt he was always just another week away from coming back home. We feel this in our everyday lives. The anxiety of the unknown. Despite not knowing exactly how we are going to get to our destination, we must hold steadfast to the reason *why* we must make it to our destination. When I'm spinning records, I know, without any doubt, I must do what I was paid to do which is *rock the party!* Believing that I will, despite any and all efforts to the contrary, requires letting go of my expectation of how every detailed aspect of how my party, just like my life, will go, and instead let God move. I didn't necessarily know how a fifth grade kid in Ms. Squire's class who hated reading would end up becoming a best-selling author. Or could I guess the route it would take for a jewelry clerk at Kohl's department store to sell millions of copies of books or move from checking and saving accounts to learning the complex profession of investment advising, especially having emerged from poverty.

F.E.A.R. (Forget Everything And Rise)

Fear, arrogance, or a combination of both can prevent us from radically trusting the process we are undergoing called maturation. We must ride the wave we created and that was created for us. When things are smooth, some of us think it couldn't possibly be going so well. Consequently, we self-sabotage and revert to step one of picking a tempo again, but remember, it's always easier to *pick a tempo* than it is to *drop your first record, feel the beat,* or *ride the wave.* Don't go back to what feels good. Oftentimes, we regress or take two steps backward, after taking three steps forward. Without a doubt, this first happens in our minds. We trick ourselves because we're scared of the reality and self-accountability of success. Luckily, we can transcend this cycle. When truly locked into fearlessness and knowing there is no alternative to success, we focus our energy on gratitude, and we can relax enough to ride along the frequency of faith and the wavelength of success. As an eagle rides the air streams, as a DJ smoothly blends into his next track, we must move like water over rocks.

DON'T LOVE YOUR DAY JOB? LOVE YOUR DAYDREAM.

Arrogance is the thief of time. We can also self-sabotage by wasting our most precious resource — time. I don't subscribe to the get-rich-quick, internet philosophy because it forces one to compare their life's journey to that of others. It also preoccupies our time with the business of others, instead of our own business. When we don't humble ourselves to learn in every environment we're in, we waste life away. *Think And Grow Rich* by Napoleon Hill explains how every negative experience carries with it "a seed of equivalent positive benefit". This is possible after any happenstance because by personal experience we learn through kinetics, creating muscle memory yielding compound intelligence, which is the act of making less mistakes over time. I don't believe you should quit your day job until you can live a sustainable lifestyle on an alternative source of income. Instead, unlike most entrepreneurs, my methodology is you don't have to love your day job, but you must be absolutely empathic about your daydream. Allow me to explain.

When I worked as a cashier or in a cell phone store, I knew that wasn't where my party ended. My career wasn't in that industry. I needed a job, after moving home from a failed attempt at living in Miami. I simply needed to get on my feet. I knew I would not retire from the work I did daily at the store. I did not love my day job, but my daydream remained my compass. The vision I had for my life did not conclude with me selling iPhones and tablets. However, how did I walk into the store owning just a flip phone and leave as a top-three salesman of connected devices between three neighboring states? How did I take a part-time job as a production assistant at a conservative FOX news station, despite being a liberal President Obama supporter? How did I work as a bank teller, doing nothing more than depositing transactions and move to managing millions of dollars of retirement assets? It's due to the power of intense belief. I knew where I was at the time wasn't where I'd end up. I believed something *greater* than me had something *bigger* for me, and I walked with that radical trust, no matter what. I didn't waste my time complaining about how I hated my job. I loved my dream enough to find good in every work experience that was not my destiny, so no time was wasted. The double up.

With every job I've had, I've sifted through the mud like a gold miner, seeking even just the smallest piece of gold I could find. In every experience, I found a skill I could hone in that moment that would serve my ultimate purpose later in life, just as a DJ selects certain songs, playing them in a strategic order, to incite a crowd. In this same fashion, we must *ride the wave* in the music of life, taking each singular song, blending the best parts of them together, weaving in and out of different life experiences and creating a melodic stream of existence. We are the culmination of excellence, like a seamless DJ set. Ever gone to a concert or show and the DJ seemed to know what song you were thinking next? Then suddenly, boom! They drop the record you had in mind? That's connection. We must create an image of our life by a tapestry of different songs. That's radical trust. Blend the beats. You will survive.

Your daydream is on your vision board created in chapter one where you also you *picked your tempo.* Remember, this is the life you most deeply desire and for which you are inherently wired to achieve. This fusion of images serves as the bedrock for which you live your life, and I suggest updating it once every season. Our daydream creates peace of mind, evokes clarity of vision, and moves us closer to self-actualization. It is okay to not love your day job, but don't forfeit your daydream. If you're wondering where your dreams are, open the portal to your heart because that's where they live. *Dreams Are Made To Be Achieved* ™.

OPEN THE PORTAL TO YOUR HEART

My deepest dreams are rooted in my desire to live a life comparable to my deceased father. My deepest pain points me toward my deepest source of empathy and connection. My dreams are proportionally related to my deepest areas of pain. The ways in my life I desire to be a resource to humanity are inextricably linked to the songs in my life. Let no experience be of insignificant value, or else, you've willfully wasted time. Would you prefer to rock your own party or give the gig to someone else? When life throws you bad records, do you trust yourself enough to still *ride the wave*?

I have overcome the following 7 F.E.A.Rs in my life:

1.

2.

3.

4.

5.

6.

7.

Overcoming these fears makes me feel:

_____

_____

_____

_____

_____

_____

_____

Based on conquering these feelings, can I overcome future fears? (Circle One)

Yes/No

5

KEEP SPINNING HITS

Consistency - (n) agreement or harmony of parts or features to one another or a whole

As we get comfortable in our mix and gain a rapport with our audience, they know our style and trust our sonic leadership by rocking with us, so we must *keep spinning hit records*! We must not give up on ourselves through the vicissitudes of life. Expect to be a troubleshooter and find long-term fixes for short-term challenges. Keeping hits on your turntables is your main concern in this phase of life. For me, this is the part of every party when I have an extended set of dropping the most popular songs back to back! This hit-dropping fury can last for hours or a few minutes, depending on if the event is a wedding or a corporate event. The length of the set also makes a difference. More than likely, your hits section demands hours of your set or the majority of it.

KEEP CUTTIN'

In this space of harmonious agreements in our friendships, work-ships, and kinships, we are challenged to residually show up in excellence. The fact that we must keep being our greatest selves activates such God-like ability to do so. As people, we can choose our destiny. Unlike most animals, we can choose how our story ends. We have a stake in our existence and are conscious of it. We show gratitude for our lives daily when we complete our morning routine, write our vision and repeat our dream statement seven times daily. Our consistency sets us apart from other DJs who may only have a few hits prepared for the night. We have a lot more than a few; in fact, we have an abundant supply. We will not give up our chance to tell our story through our own mix. So we keep spinning. When life does it's best to knock you off your square, keep spinning. Know that you are protected by a force greater than any person could ever be. You are borrowing energy from the Ultimate Creator to inform your brushstrokes on a canvas. In this flow state, it's predetermined where you will drop the beat as you cut your next record. So keep cuttin'.

We may get to a point where we feel dream anxiety. Here, our self-talk guards our progress. We stay the course, remaining on a positive wavelength because of the power in our dream statement. The presence of unexpected, inevitable challenges and unforeseen circumstances no longer dictate our enjoyment of life. We enjoy life for what it is: a gift from the Ultimate Creator. We don't panic in the face of adversity or danger because there is simply no room for failing our audience. Remember, we are performing live. In life, every take is a live take. The show must go on. Our purpose outweighs our fear. As DJs, we know fear cannot compete with purpose because purpose will win every time. We were hired to produce a memorable experience for our client. We are prepared to troubleshoot in the mix, and we remain calm while proceeding because we are tapped into the real purpose we are here, not the impeding circumstance. We make a way out of none. No microphone? Sometimes, we may hook our headphones up to the microphone input and use our headset to talk over our breaks. It's jazz in action. We improvise in ways that best serve our purpose to produce the best and most memorable experience for our clients. At your life party, what hits will be played? Your life is the party, and you are your own client. How many people will feel the beats on your dance floor?

BUILD RAPPORT THROUGH EXCELLENCE

Our best chance at gaining rapport with others is by consistently producing desired results. Just as a DJ continues to spin hits to retain your attention, you must drop hits to your audience. This distinctive skill to continue producing excellence sets you apart from your counterparts on a day job or your competitors as a business owner. Consequently, this may unintentionally incite division between you and other parties. Don't expect other people to be happy for your expansion. Your own fulfillment is your business, where you are most responsible, because here is where you have the best *ability* to *respond*. When you have what it takes, rightfully, people want to take what you have. What's easier than crafting one's own success? Just steal someone else's. Naturally, when there's a change in tempo, record, or genre of music in an open format DJ set, some listeners would rather you keep playing the same old tune. When you level up, some people would prefer you turn it down. When you get in

the mix and things are going right, a few things tend to go left. No matter the troubleshooting issue, *keep spinning hits!* Remember, think and act in a problem vs. solution binary.

At this stage in your personal development, you've

realized your true, ingenious talents in order to manifest your destiny. You know and believe your Dream Statement to be thy staff in a valley and a javelin of humility in your affluent times of consistent hits. At this point, you may now feel a sense of accomplishment. Rightfully so, especially if this is your first time ever considering yourself to be the lead architect of how your party will sound when you leave this planet. What will people say about you 400 years after you've impacted the Earth? Will they remember what you stood for, represented, or left them otherwise to survive with, especially in a world like we currently live?

SIFT & WINNOW: Find Your Piece of Gold

As DJs of our own party, we are awarded trust by God to partner in creating our best life. We can discover what we were born to do by being open-minded as a DJ. This means being prepared to switch the song when it gets boring, repetitive or monotonous. Once we've learned a skill on a new job, most young people desire growth opportunities within their industry. Despite taking new job roles an average of every eighteen to twenty-four months, young people must find what piece of gold they can in any job they currently hold. In this spirit of humility, no experience is insignificant, and no time is wasted because ultimately you are accelerating your agenda.

ACT LIKE YOU'VE BEEN HERE BEFORE

There are a few key concepts to ensuring you can *keep spinning hits* while in the mix of life. First, we must have created our vision of what the best party should sound like, matching each song accordingly. We must also have the necessary crates of organized music to perform our best. Organized action creates best results. We must have done our musical homework by listening to our records to ensure proper sound quality and that the song titles match the credited artist, before the party. Because we've seen this moment in our visualization once, we have a peculiar sensation we've been here before. This way, when we get to the venue and play, we feel like this is our second time being in the space. We experience a déjà vu that comforts us, conquering our nervousness. We've been here before, so we don't act out of character. We proceed even when plans change. In fact, that's the purpose of a plan, to have something, a blueprint you can change and rely on in a time of distress. We have our vision in our mind, and we've *dropped our first record* aligned with that vision. *Riding the wave* of continuous hits draws people toward us.

The law of attraction works most effectively in a state of peace of mind, validity, and control. The clearer our vision, and the more we keep our feelings, thoughts, words, and actions aligned with our deepest desires, the more we see the power of the universe conspiring on our behalf to manifest our dreams into reality, experiencing a heaven on Earth. When we match the frequency of the life partner we want, they appear. Not a second earlier or later. We must be ready to properly receive the gifts wrapped by life. If we're not careful, we may misperceive a blessing as a burden or mischaracterize a stepping stool as a stumbling block, mistakenly kicking it aside.

MISTAKES DON'T MAKE THE MIX

A DJ may pick a bad song during his set. They may misread the crowd and play the wrong song. In this scenario, you can recover by continuing to spin hits. Pick a song you know will give you a chance to earn your audience's affinity back. Select a tempo, drop the record, and ride the wave. Spinning hit records has become a science to you at this point. You are discovering your $85 billion worth of abstract faculties and converting them into monetary physical equivalents. Your candlelight is now captured in a filament, and your party is a lightbulb to you and others. Your peers brag about your success. Your closest friends express pride in their connection with you. Your family sees how joyful your life makes you, and you emit a natural glorious glow. To others, you look like you're shining. Your smile is rooted within gratitude. Love is radiating from your reach.

THE FLOW STATE

When we align our subconscious mind, which helps us breathe, hear, and smell during sleep, with our awake, conscious self, our party becomes unstoppable. We are in the flow state created for us

to experience by the Ultimate Creator, God. The flow state is like Prince, screaming a falsetto, falling into perfect pitch or James Brown bellowing tonal grunts in the most impeccable pattern, conversing with the drums. This is where the natural and supernatural realms agree. When a DJ is in the flow, they are fully immersed in a feeling and an energized focus, encompassed by the enjoyment of the process of playing music for others. Love your process. In this dimension, time is malleable.

THE TIME IS NOW

This is that part of every party where it either feels like you gained an extra hour or you lost time. Have you ever felt a party you attended got extended or surprisingly shortened, but time zones didn't change? This is the flow state. While we are here, we play our absolute best records because, if we've played our songs right and built enough rapport with our audience, we can usher them into the best part of the night, which is creating a moment they will most likely remember. The flow is when a DJ completely controls the energy in a space and can get people to fulfill any verbal command. Everybody put your hands up! This is where you make this music-playing thing look easy, having people think almost anybody can do it. But because you remember the nights of painstaking practice and the hours you invested into listening to your records, organizing your playlists, perfecting mixes you thought about throughout the day, you know you are in an elite class of professional static selectors who people pay to party with. I hope you're charging the right price. At this time, the music reigns supreme, and the crowd submits to your will and expertise as their beloved DJ. Go DJ!

In life, your crowd is your loved ones. The people watching you live your best life are your audience. They are the people who cheer for you. You are the expert on your life. What hit records will keep spinning for you when you have transitioned back to where we all came from before we were born? Will your DJ set be unique to your story or simply a copy of what you heard on the radio of life? Will you attempt to replicate another DJ's sound, misusing your time trying to imitate their style, or will you leave your own sound stamp on the world? Will people know you for the evidence of goodness you left behind and the stories others can tell about their personal experience with you, or will your one party become a party of one?

Continually spinning hits is what we all must do to get people on our dance floor. We will not fill our dance floor with dead air or silence. Speak your dreams into existence, write your vision, craft your dream vision board, draft your Dream Statement, and most importantly, align your actions with the desires of your heart.

CREATE A MORNING ROUTINE

Having a morning routine is a sure way to *keep spinning hits* in your life. By starting your day with a healthy workout, playing good music, reading, eating breakfast, meditating, and taking time for yourself, before the day gets under way is a method many impactful global leaders have used to repower themselves daily. Since life is guaranteed to produce unpredictability, making sure a portion of your day is predictable, therefore controllable, you satisfy your natural daily dietary need for peace of mind. When this peace is juxtaposed against things not going your way throughout the day, you have a frame of reference where you've controlled what you could already for the day. This relaxes you. We naturally want to know what's next in our lives or how to make our dreams come true. A daily routine, coupled with writing your vision daily for fifteen minutes just before you retire at night and speaking your dream statement with conviction seven times throughout your day, gives you the momentum you need. When we do this, we feel in control of our destiny, living offensively versus merely responding to challenges. We retain our strength and manifest our dreams because we direct our thoughts, feelings, words, attitudes and actions for the day, with tenacious autonomy and precise intention. Just as a DJ would feel in control during a live event, we are in control of our efforts, starting with our morning. Every morning, turn yourself up. Amplify your existence! Get on the frequency of the life you most deeply desire, and it will key into your channel in return.

If I created my best life-party, I would feel:

_____
_____
_____

6

FEEL THE DANCE FLOOR

Build A Dream Circle Around Your Business

Byron Katie, author of *Loving What Is*, writes there are only three businesses: your business, God's business, and other people's business. She contends, if you're focused on other people's business or God's business, who's working on yours? Of the three, we can only control our business. God's business, how we were born, our identity, our race, gender, religion or cultural norms were, for the most part, gifted to us as who we are. It's our unique identity. Just as we can't blame our identity for making us fall short of our destiny, we can't become so consumed with the opinions, lifestyle and choices of others that we fall delinquent in building a party on our own dance floor. Our business is our responsibility. Our destiny, our purpose, our immediate family, our life's work, and our party are all our business. Everything else is not.

When you're building a monument of success and you reach the apex, you crown your structure with its final pieces. Yet what good does it profit a person to build a custom home, complete with gold-plated toilet seats, granite countertops, million-dollar art, marble floors, and gold door handles, with termites eating the wood in the basement? What good does it do a family for their lifestyle to exist on a crack in the foundation of their pyramid of success? Our primary efforts during this segment of our journey demand that we surround ourselves with the best quality people of the highest character with our best interest at the core of their relationship with us in order for us to prosper, reaching new dimensions.

MAKE LIFE DANCE FOR YOU

We must inspire our tribe to gather around us in a circle of support and get them to join us on the dance floor of life. Our audience must fill the dance floor, whereas we, as the performance DJ, must actually *feel the dance floor.* I dance when I spin records because it informs me if my audience is feeling me. If I'm dancing, chances are they are as well. I don't get distracted with dancing, but I make sure I'm feeling the groove. If I am, I know from how I'm moving what my audience is doing. I may only take a glimpse a few times at what they're doing besides when I'm engaging them on the microphone or demanding an interactive call and response. Your tribe is comprised of your advocates, family, and closest friends. Connect with them and get them to fill your dance floor first. Others will follow.

DRAW YOUR DREAM CIRCLE

Building your Dream Circle of committed supporters creates a solid foundation of fearless networking. As your career develops or company grows, you will need to ensure your brand, as well as your social footprint, aligns with your audience's values. How do consumers feel about your product or service? Give your early adapters a reward or thank you for their belief in you. Your Dream Circle is your protective space where you can experiment with creativity, absent of judgment or ridicule, only constructive feedback. If you want to be an impactful creative, you must be precise in your intentions. Your genius will require protection, developmental resources, investment, nourishment, and time to manifest. In fact, some dreams take longer to realize, depending on their complexity and size. Your dream isn't dependent upon that of others. Your dream is connected to others, yet it remains independent. It is your dream only, no one else's. This highlights the need for you to build a trusted group of souls around you as your principled circle of influence. This is your Dream Circle. Tribal support stimulates a communal mastermind, sparked out of a high thought-frequency. Getting a group of people to focus their collective energy and intentions on protecting you with love and supporting your sustainability helps you reach levels of creative insights you would have not otherwise experienced alone. Because of this scientific fact, you must align your tribe with your vision. You must assemble your Dream Circle of personal avengers who support you in building your most successful life-party.

Dale Carnegie explains your need to win friends, influence people, and draw the best out of others. Life, like DJing music, is a collaborative process. As a DJ, I rely on a producer, sound engineer, and artist to create a mood with which I experiment in a room full of strangers. I'm in a constant state of partnership, negotiation, and collaboration with, at least, five other people when I'm working behind the turntables. Just as a successful DJ must work directly and indirectly with a team, you must assemble your tribe of personal, trusted board of advisors.

Your advisors can be either spiritually intact or live in present day. It's your choice. My spiritual cabinet is comprised of deceased members only, while my living Dream Circle tribe members are the most important people to me over time. As a part of my morning routine, I access both mastermind groups and tap into their wisdom. For a spiritual connection, I meditate, take a moment to connect with my ancestors, and consult them with my challenges at the time. It's not dark or demonic in any fashion. I simply close my eyes and envision myself sitting at the head of a roundtable of cabinet members, and they all come in one by one, except James Brown and Ida B. Wells. Prince and Michael Jackson usually make very grand, individual entrances. There are others with a seat at the table as well.

I ask them their opinions on ideas I have, concepts I've created, or hunches I have, over time. I imagine what they will say to me in their unique voices, which I've come to learn by way of the character in their life's work. These consecrated cultural icons connect with me and posthumously offer guided meditation.

Contrarily, my physical Dream Circle seems to me to be handpicked for me by God. They are the people I call upon during an emergency or epiphany. Some have known me my entire life, and others have met me during significant points in my life. The key is they are all there for me. My advisors are unconditional pillars of support in everything I build.

IT'S YOUR PEROGATIVE

God places these people in your life as you mature. They fill your dance floor. In fact, your personal tribe is the group of pre-party friends that come and stay for the after party also. Imagine life as a garden. You must cultivate it and design how that garden looks. The seeds you plant in your personal garden of excellence are completely your choice. Just as it is a DJ's prerogative to include the song selections for their set organized in a crate, or a horticulturalist may pick the seeds to plant in a garden, you must decide on which connections you value most. Who has your radical trust? Who do you most desire to take with you on your journey? Who do you want rooted in your garden?

Think Like A DJ

The goal is to get to a point where you'll be cued with so many hits that you will be able to keep dropping them one after another. Your Dream Circle helps you determine what a hit sounds like. From here, your Dream Circle will begin to identify the specific thematic elements of your DJing style that match the consistencies among their collective lifestyles. Your audience will dance with you. Ultimately, the crowd you've built through an arduous labor of love will become a culture.

DO IT FOR THE CULTURE

Culture is meaning plus people. When I lived on an American Indian reservation for a week, I learned this definition of culture from a respected elder woman named Ada Deer. In order to build a significant understanding and bonding among people, we must bond ourselves in radical trust. Just as "M" is for money, we must trust that, when we pull up to the bank of life, we will cash a check marked "sufficient funds."

When I went to the corner store as a kid, Jimmy, the old Black man behind the counter, would give me 100 pieces of penny candy any time I had 100 pennies. True value. We must make the deposits in ourselves that will afford us the opportunity to make equal and opposite withdrawals. We must pay our future successful selves today. Our lives are the best party we've ever heard of, and we will meet thousands of people throughout our existence. They should dance to our music. We can play a beat to our own drum, but only for so long. In our efforts to fill the dance floor, we must galvanize those in the vicinity of our sounds to dance. How do you want to move people? What impact do you want to have on your Dream Circle, the people you share core values, frequencies and meaning with? What's the culture of your dance floor?

DIVERSIFY YOUR DANCE FLOOR

Diversity in life works just like it does in your investment portfolio and in your song selection as a DJ, beautifully. When creatives and business owners build organic cultures from an in-group of early adapters, they have the opportunity to steer their ark. Who's on your ark? Who's populating your dance floor, and who was at the pre-party that'll still be with you during the after party?

HEAR ALL THE VOICES

One of the most important aspects of creating a culture is listening to the voices in the room. To be a successful DJ, you must hear all the voices in the room. When I spin high school proms, graduations, or homecomings, I typically request a Spotify playlist of "must plays" from my clients.

Furthermore, when I produce entertainment for a wedding client, I schedule a few meetings with my clients to simply talk about the kind of music they love and their personal love story. I want my mix to match the mood of each client's vision. I listen to them. There's no powerful, memorable party, without listening to those you serve. Not only must you listen to their voices, you must observe their kinetics and body language. If there are people dancing, that is a good sign. If people look like they're ordering a drink from a hard to read coffeehouse menu, then, maybe, you should just change the song. Pick a new tempo, drop another record, ride the wave, keep spinning hits and your dance floor will replenish itself by way of manifestation and the law of attraction. When we listen and respond with humility and direction, we are more likely to build a tribe rich with open mindedness. Inclusive excellence is our strength. We are by no means, as one person, all God's glory. In an ensemble of fine-tuned horns, we can still be a Miles Davis trumpet. Listen for your voice and how it embraces the voices of others to whom you have a tribal connection. Catch the rhythm, play in sync.

As a DJ, one of our greatest gifts is the ability to predict and improvise. Our profession itself is jazz. We create safe atmospheres for people to express themselves through movement. We also craft organic cultures from an epicenter of like-mindedness. Think about your favorite DJ. Although you may have never met them, you feel as though you know their taste. You are part of their Dream Circle. Who's a part of your tribe? Who will be on the boat with you in retirement? You only live once. Will your one party be a party of one? As a jazz drummer rides the hi-hats, you can pick a tempo, one that a like-minded listener can identify and trust in the midst of the inevitable improvisation accompanying life. We want to fill our dance floor with people who tell others about their memorable experience with us. We want to take clients and make them fans, convert our fans into friends, and then into family. Family unequivocally advocates for you. Family is your tribe. Fill your dance floor with the people closest to you and be sure to show up to their party as well.

LISTEN TO YOURSELF: DISCERNMENT

When you're building your tribe and fearlessly networking, you must use discernment to vet beneficial opportunities from subtractive detours. Deciding which partnerships are in your best interest requires acumen. When feeling like a bad song blend or like you have a bad taste in your mouth because you can't decide who's for you and who's merely with you, recite your Dream Statement. From here, your vision board will repaint itself across the projector in your mind's eye. Who do you see there with you in your vision? Does the business deal on the table or job opportunity in front of you align with your long-term goal to *rock the party*? Is your mission aligned with the outcomes of this opportunity? Do you see yourself getting closer to a maximum celebration in your life-party with what's presented, or does it turn your decibels down? If necessary, you have your Dream Circle and your audience's feedback to help answer these questions. In Jay-Z words, "What's better than one billionaire?"

DON'T CHASE, ATTRACT YOUR DREAM

In your pursuit to build your Dream Circle around your business, don't lose your goals to the wishes of others. Attract your dream; don't chase it. Be what your dream wants, and you will obtain the lifestyle you most deeply desire. Become a healthy dwelling place for your dream. Be healthy soil for it to be planted. What do you want people to remember most about your life-party? Others could potentially have a lasting effect on your party. Vetting who to include in your dream and who to delete takes courage and pivotal decision-making.

When I first started a partnership with a college friend of mine, I didn't expect it would result in me having to swim against the stream to keep a positive reputation after he took money and bailed out of town unexpectedly. Although our disbandment never went public or made it to social media, other business owners we'd both partnered with as a unit echoed many of the same financial business issues I'd had with him. This failed partnership ultimately impacted my relationships going forward, forcing me to rebuild them in a more solid, authentic fashion. I was forced to spend my most precious asset, time, something I can't get back, unlike the money he took. Nonetheless, business got done and more records were spun.

Like a record on a turntable, life will take you for a spin, so what music do you want people to sing when your life is over? Protect yourself with the Dream Circle you've built.

Encompass yourself. Solidify your culture on the dance floor. After you've spent time cementing your reputation in a course room, at your job or your own business in the marketplace, you are positioned to *rock the party*! You are your own client, DJing your celebration. Who's showing up to rejoice with you on your dance floor?

7

ROCK THE PARTY

"Leadership is impact." - Martinez White

To *rock your party*, you have to be a sound scientist. You must've done your homework by listening this whole time. If you skipped a step, you must return to where you last found success and start playing tunes from there. You are not permitted to disconnect from any progressive step before proceeding any further in the seven proven chronological steps in this book. If you do, you will not reap the fully calculated returns. *Rocking a party* is impossible without preparation and being familiar with the ultimate vision for you and your Dream Circle. You must have a destination for this lakeside ship. Daily, we must connect with our inner, creative voice through the technique of our creative morning routine. Clarity of vision will dictate the definition of the brushstrokes in your painted vision. You have the power to extract realities from your imagination, creating a physical equivalent of anything you wish to manifest. Even if it takes you seven times to repeat. Recall, you are in the DJ booth of your life-party, rocking your own custom mix. No matter the obstacle, you're keeping the movement going because you must. You are performing live.

Self-care is your foundation, creating peace of mind. Give yourself the best holistic understanding of who you are by spending time with yourself. Julia Cameron, author of *The Artist's Way: A Spiritual Path to Higher Creativity*, demands you to take yourself on artist dates. Watch a movie alone, see a show or participate in a new activity by yourself. Listen to your soul. Take time weekly to unplug from the business of others or God, and refill your reservoir of creativity with deposits of creative water. Don't go thirsty. Give yourself the best shot at success by getting in position for what's to come. Your marvel is your art. You must protect & expand it. You are interstellar and awe-inspiring altogether. Be your own best advocate. It's okay to play to ensure you fairly win. When you win, your Dream Circle will be there to celebrate you. They will surely keep you in the win zone. Because you *kept spinning hit records*, eventually the dance floor filled, and people close to you witnessed the actualization of your life purpose. A true party, never seen before, that surpasses even your wildest dreams.

You're the captain of the ship of riches. Your vision and God's vision make for a third understanding, a mastermind connection. Once your freewill aligns with God's purpose for your life, you will be onto stability and upward economic ascendance. Your words, thoughts, feelings, emotions, attitude and actions will align, manifesting your dream vision.

Self-knowledge is the root of connectedness. We build the capacity to do more in our lives, through sharpening the tools in our toolkit. We must have extra cables, additional batteries, back-up hard drives, and personal contacts if we get in a compromised situation while responding to the needs of a large group of others in a real-time environment. We are conductors of the night. We orchestrate the festivities. We've first seen our party in our visualization before it became practical and real. The essence of our lives will emerge from the roots of our experiences. Are your roots deep enough in order to withstand the looming, inevitable wind?

YOUR PARTY, YOUR PURPOSE

Our party is connected to our purpose. It may be a challenge to automatically know your purpose. Most people don't. It should get you excited that, because of this fact, if you do know your purpose, you graduate to an enlightened existence during your natural life. When we know ourselves, and God has revealed our purpose to us, we bring more people to the party by showing them the light. In addition, we help make more people whole, living and walking in their divine destiny. In this creative space, you exist between a peaceful place of discovering new things and the diligence of fulfilling an order of purpose. Fidelity to your mission is your prize. Your win is actionable faith, acting in your purpose.

Feel the excitement of *rocking your party*, especially since life is in constant rotation. What we see now may not always exist. A successful DJ must live in the moment, occupying a selective space in the sublime. Can you connect to a yoga nidra flow state in the mix of your lifestyle? Perhaps you can do it during your morning routine? Even the planet you currently sit on is revolving around the sun. Our world itself is spinning on an axis. Life is always moving. Although things may not be perfect, just like our counterintuitively-leaning planet, we must exceed the awkward and still get our RSVP list to overflow. The party must go on.

Rocking the party is about living your best life. It is indescribable, like mom's smile on Mother's Day because of your gift. The flow isn't overbearing; it's easy, like Sunday morning. When your life-party has been planned, with expected troubleshooting issues, you have the ingredients for an event to be reckoned with. Throughout your brief years on this planet, you get the opportunity to live a life to be proud of and abundantly share. A true leader desires impact. They possess an inherent desire to create joy and fruitful experiences for others. DJs are some of the most impactful people in our lives. When COVID-19 struck the world, so did DJs. Music can't be cancelled because it's how our soul sounds. Our feelings are dissected and dispersed in song. When people hear music at your life-party, can you guarantee the floor will fill and hearts will overflow?

When you exercise actionable faith and align your emotions, thoughts, words, actions and attitudes with the picturization of your most successful party, the universe conspires on your behalf. When your vision is enacted, your turntable starts to spin. As soon as you begin to write your vision daily and repeat your dream statement seven times, your record is in rotation. Soon, you will have a heightened sense of awareness. Comparable to when you buy a new car and suddenly you seem to notice it everywhere. Because you are tuned into the wavelength of success, everything that is on that same frequency of faith starts to become attracted to you, and you notice it. In this flow state, you still labor to get ahead and work hard, but it will become quite clear that what you're seeking is also searching for you. The right people, connections, networks, opportunities, and second chances will become self-evident. More people will fill your dance floor, and your one party will properly represent your most successful life.

The truth is we all have the capacity to manifest the person we were all individually designed to be. Our cinderblock values, core virtues, morals, ethics and beliefs become our perfected art. As naturally creative beings, we produce the motion pictures on our projector every day. What images are in your movie? Will people be able to learn from your scenes? Furthermore, are your music mixes inspiring others to dance?

THINKING LIKE A DJ

Making the decision to be a DJ has been one of the most rewarding decisions of my life. DJing informs my thinking process and gives me a framework for life. The autonomy and freedom of thought gifted to a jock equips the DJ with a remarkable peace of mind. You have freewill to choose your destiny. Just as a DJ chooses the outcome of an event, you have significant dominion over the results of your life.

Remember, you are your own client and your life is the party. If you know *"Dreams Are Made To Be Achieved"* ™, what's your dream? Define it. An obstacle to ever reaching the highest height of success in your life can be your desire to take shortcuts or quick routes. One of my Kenyan professors explained, it's not often that things that come like the wind don't also go just like it. Don't self-sabotage your own life event due to laziness and cheating to get ahead. In the presence of adversity, stand strong and deliver. Don't shake, wade or wither.

You are the dream of your ancestors. Your Dream Circle is depending on you to host the party of your life and leave an intergenerational legacy. Your last name will mean something. Your character will advance humanity. As a DJ, you impact culture by helping people be more of their natural selves. Your intent to get others dancing in the direction of joy will draw favorable connections toward you in this lifetime, while earning gratitude from your Creator in the next. You will be rewarded for your display of love for all mankind. Your scholarship of self and stewardship to others, through the power in your gift, will create intergenerational karma for your family tree. Like my little brother Zeek's clothing line slogan proclaims,

"Family Above All." The quality of our lives will be reflected in the quality of the lives of those we impact. Your children will, one day, ask to spin at the turntables of life, talk on the microphone, or play with the crossfader, you had better discover what it takes to rock your own successful life-party by then.

Rocking the party is what we all want. How we do it is in our total control. No trip starts without a destination. In order to lead others, you must first know where you're going. Think to a time

when you felt completely at ease with an experience yet deeply contemplative about its meaning. Maybe you experienced this after walking across the graduation stage, receiving good news from a job for which you persisted, the person you're dating said "I love you" for the first time, or you found out you were about to have your firstborn child. This same feeling of boundless, striking awe will be your experience at your own life-party. Weightlessness.

The specific experiences it takes to arrive at this point of living out our dreams may be different for everyone, yet the seven principals of spinning our poverty into prosperity are steadfast, tried and proven. Ideas may develop over time, yet principals hold to be everlasting. Here, you have a blueprint for success. Because you've learned the strategic formula in this book, you are one of few who are well-versed in the methods of manifestation, self-actualization, how to use the law of attraction to draw wealth, and ultimately how to truly *Think Like A DJ.*

I look forward to attending your party. Are you planning to come to mine?

OUTRO

"REPEAT ROTATION"

"Freedom is the continuous action we all must take, and each generation must do its part to create an even more fair, more just society." - U.S. Congressman John Lewis

The great management guru Peter Drucker once said, "there is no success without a successor." When we transition and our life party has concluded, we must pack our bags and go. The difference in real life is we don't get the opportunity to unplug or break down our equipment. Oftentimes, we transition without forewarning.

Because our party can be cut short, without any notice, we must discover a way to incessantly repeat our successful festivity, by leaving behind a blueprint for those we love. We've dedicated our every effort to learning how to *rock our party*, but in order to have residual success, we must teach our wisdom to the next generations in our family.

We must lay a solid foundation of managed risk, wealth accumulation and financial freedom. Our success alone, in one generation, is insufficient to claim full victory.

We must forever rotate the turntables, launching into the next song because the beat goes on.

Repeat these proven seven steps often as a philosophy of success. In this one generation, set up the next two generations for upward economic mobility. Poverty was only yours to peep. May prosperity be yours to keep.

"Dreams Are Made To Be Achieved"™

7 STEPS TO SPIN POVERTY INTO PROSPERITY

1. PICK A TEMPO – Make A Decision. Write Your Vision. Create Your Dream Statement. Craft Your Vision Board
2. DROP YOUR FIRST RECORD – Act On Faith
3. FEEL THE BEAT – Connect With Likeminded Individuals
4. RIDE THE WAVE – Radically Trust Yourself
5. KEEP SPINNING HITS - Consistently Connect & Create A Morning Routine
6. FEEL THE DANCEFLOOR – Build A Dream Circle Around Your Business, Fearlessly Network, Assemble Your Personal Advisory Board
7. ROCK THE PARTY – Leave An Intergenerational Legacy

ABOUT THE AUTHOR

Martinez White, Emmy Award recipient, founding member of the Wisconsin Association of Black Men and CEO of Intuition Productions, upholds the belief that *"Dreams Are Made To Be Achieved"* **™**. As a member of Alpha Phi Alpha Fraternity, Inc., White's mission is to empower one billion people to join his Dream Circle by self-actualizing their dreams & living their most abundant destiny.

Living in Mombasa, Kenya and volunteering at Alica Keys' Keep A Child Alive campaign's BOMU Medical Center, fighting the HIV/AIDS pandemic forever changed White's world perspective. As a licensed in- vestment advisor, White teaches clients how to create intergenerational financial freedom, regardless of socioeconomic class. He believes *artre-preneurship*, the monetization of artistic gifts, is the best defense against institutionalized racism.

Based on this belief, at just sixteen years old, White emerged from a single-parent home of six children in

Milwaukee, Wisconsin. Against all odds, White earned his Bachelor of Arts in Communication Arts and Afro-American Studies from the University of Wisconsin-Madison, as a PEOPLE and Chancellor's Scholar at a mere twenty years old. A DJ, filmmaker, and author, White inspires us all through the power of his un- paralleled style of multimedia storytelling.

"If You Want It Done Right, Get M. White"™

ABOUT INTUITION PRODUCTIONS

Intuition Productions is a multimedia edutainment & millennial event production company. Our purpose is to produce and market music experiences, art and literary content that uplifts, enlightens, and inspires global, diverse audiences, ultimately pushing culture forward.

FIND ME ON SOCIAL MEDIA

FACEBOOK: INTUITION PRODUCTIONS

INSTAGRAM: @DJMWHITE

TWITTER/SNAPCHAT:@MRMORETHANADJ
www.martinezwhite.com

ABOUT MOTIVATIONAL M.D. PUBLISHING

Motivational M.D. Publishing is a family-owned business founded by award winning author, public health physician, and speaker Dr. Jasmine Zapata that helps musical artists, poets, and aspiring authors publish books that amplify their message, empower others, and generate additional revenue streams. By fusing the power of book publishing, music and motivation, Motivational M.D. Publishing helps authors create movements that heal, uplift, and inspire!

Connect with Motivational M.D. Publishing at
http://imreadytolaunch.com

THANK YOU TO THE FOLLOWING SUPPORTERS FOR MAKING MY FIRST BOOK POSSIBLE

Dr. Jasmine Zapata
Christina Vue
Jess Wilde
Quilen Blackwell
Dupree Armon
Iesha Armon
T.S. Banks
Lauren Morris
Tim Cole
Simone Lawrence
Keon Hutson
Shibon Patterson
Marissa Quinn Aravena
Dr. Alexander Gee, Jr.
Ananda Mirilli
Allie Lamb
Amakie Amattey
Gino Salomone
Anitra Tatum
Montae Foots
Brianna Abobora
Tyrus Cartwright
Jessica Regele
Allie Gardner
William Paul Thomas
Keith Jackson
Donovan Cotton
Read Eldred

7 RECOMMENDED READS

Think And Grow Rich - Napoleon Hill

Think And Grow Rich: A Black Choice - Dr. Dennis Kimbro

The Secret - Rhonda Byrne

The Four Agreements - Don Miguel Ruiz

Crush It!: Why NOW Is the Time to Cash in on Your Passion - Gary Vaynerchuk

Bank On You - Jeremiah J. Brown

Loving What Is - Byron Katie

DREAM PAGES:

Think Like A DJ

Think Like A DJ

Think Like A DJ

Think Like A DJ

Made in the USA
Monee, IL
31 August 2020

40641621R00059